Scotland's most exciting example of 21st Century engineering, The Falkirk Wheel, is more than just the World's first rotating boatlift. It is a symbol heralding the dawn of Britain's new canal age.

The boatlift's role may be simple, but its shape is far from conventional. In combining art and engineering, the Wheel's designers have produced a dramatic moving sculpture.

Its architecture has been likened to double-headed Celtic axes, or a vast propeller symbolic of Glasgow's shipbuilding era. Yet whatever your imagination sees, The Falkirk Wheel is already Scotland's most recognisable Monument to the Future.

As the Wheel turns, water and boats - contained in its two large gondolas - are transferred between an aqueduct linked to the upper Union Canal and a basin feeding to the adjacent Forth & Clyde Canal, 25 metres below.

Yet this dramatic looking structure performs another vital link. It reconnects, after a 70 year gap, the country's two leading Lowland Canals, both rescued from many decades of accelerating neglect.

In an ambitious scheme led by British Waterways, these once proud industrial canals have been restored and reopened to create a 'corridor of opportunity' for the future.

The project, called The Millennium Link, offers not only a direct waterway route between Edinburgh and Glasgow, but also a coast to coast connection linking the rivers Forth and Clyde.

The prime aim is to encourage new canalside development and leisure activities across the whole of the country's central belt. It will unlock even more of Scotland's potential while, at the same time, celebrate the engineering achievements of our ancestors.

How, though, was this mammoth reconstruction scheme achieved in half the time originally planned?

And how can a row of different sized cogs help turn the vast 1800 tonne Falkirk Wheel using only the same power as six kettles?

This guide provides the answers as it tells the story of a project that offers both the canal network's only white knuckle ride and a new waterway for a new Millennium.

The Millennium Link - a corridor of opportunity

Creation of Britain's largest, most ambitious canal restoration scheme, The Millennium Link, has involved repair or reconstruction work on many of its 500 structures - including bridges, locks and aqueducts - along the total 112km length of Scotland's two major Lowland Canals; the Union and the Forth & Clyde.

Sections of new canal have been cut through Edinburgh's suburbs. Long buried locks have been unearthed near Glasgow, to the surprise of local residents. New bridges have been built and original crossings refurbished.

In just three years of hectic reconstruction, rotting lock gates and stretches of abandoned stagnant canal - boasting little more than dumped supermarket trolleys and old tyres - have been transformed into 21st Century waterways, linked by the magnificent 35 metre high Falkirk Wheel.

The scheme, dubbed 'The People's Project', now offers visitors sea to sea boating facilities and links by water Scotland's premier cities Edinburgh and Glasgow. Its towpaths provide unrivalled walking and cycling opportunities, while the entire route plays host to a wealth of varied wildlife and protected rare plants that have survived, despite - and perhaps in some cases because of - its neglected years.

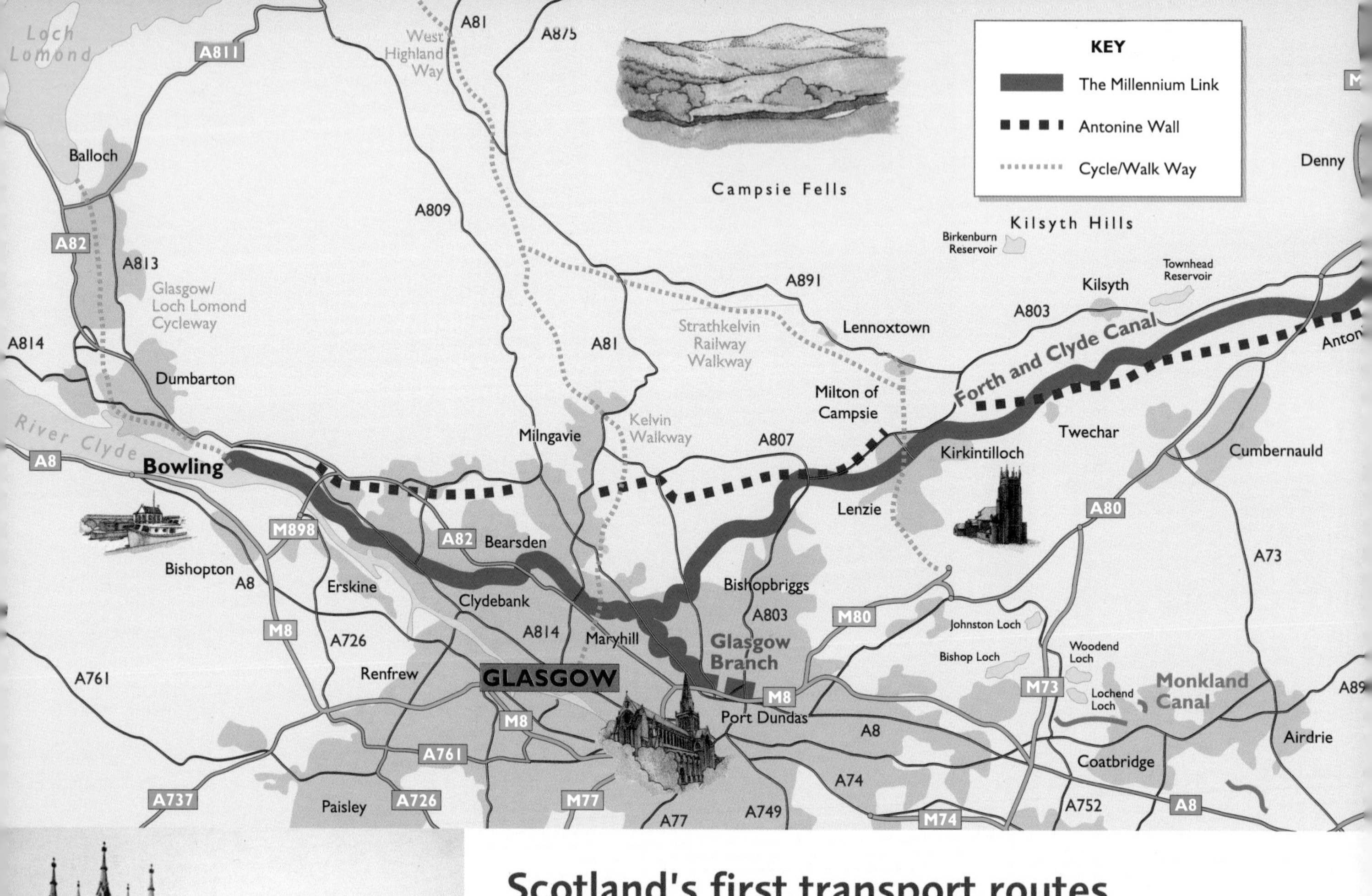

Scotland's first transport routes

The Millennium Link Project has refurbished two major canals; the 61km long Forth & Clyde and the Union Canal, originally 51km. They are connected by The Falkirk Wheel where the Union Canal has been lengthened by 2km.

Scotland's oldest canal, The Forth & Clyde - originally known as The Great Canal - runs 57km coast to coast between the ports of Bowling on the Clyde and Grangemouth on the Firth of Forth, with a 4km spur into Glasgow.

The link between Grangemouth and Glasgow was completed in 1777, offering the city a direct connection with the sea and trade with the Baltic, Scandinavia and Holland. The route from Glasgow, west to the Clyde, opened 13 years later, creating the World's first sea to sea ship canal. A major shipping centre rapidly became established at Port Dundas in the centre of Glasgow, with a wealth of goods - even whisky from the Western Isles - featured on the trading manifests.

Scotland's famous West Coast puffers, many built in the canal's own half dozen inland boatyards, became a common sight ferrying their cargoes between the central belt and outer islands.

The 1822 Union Canal has no locks along its main length. Known as a contour canal, it was built by engineer Hugh Baird all on one

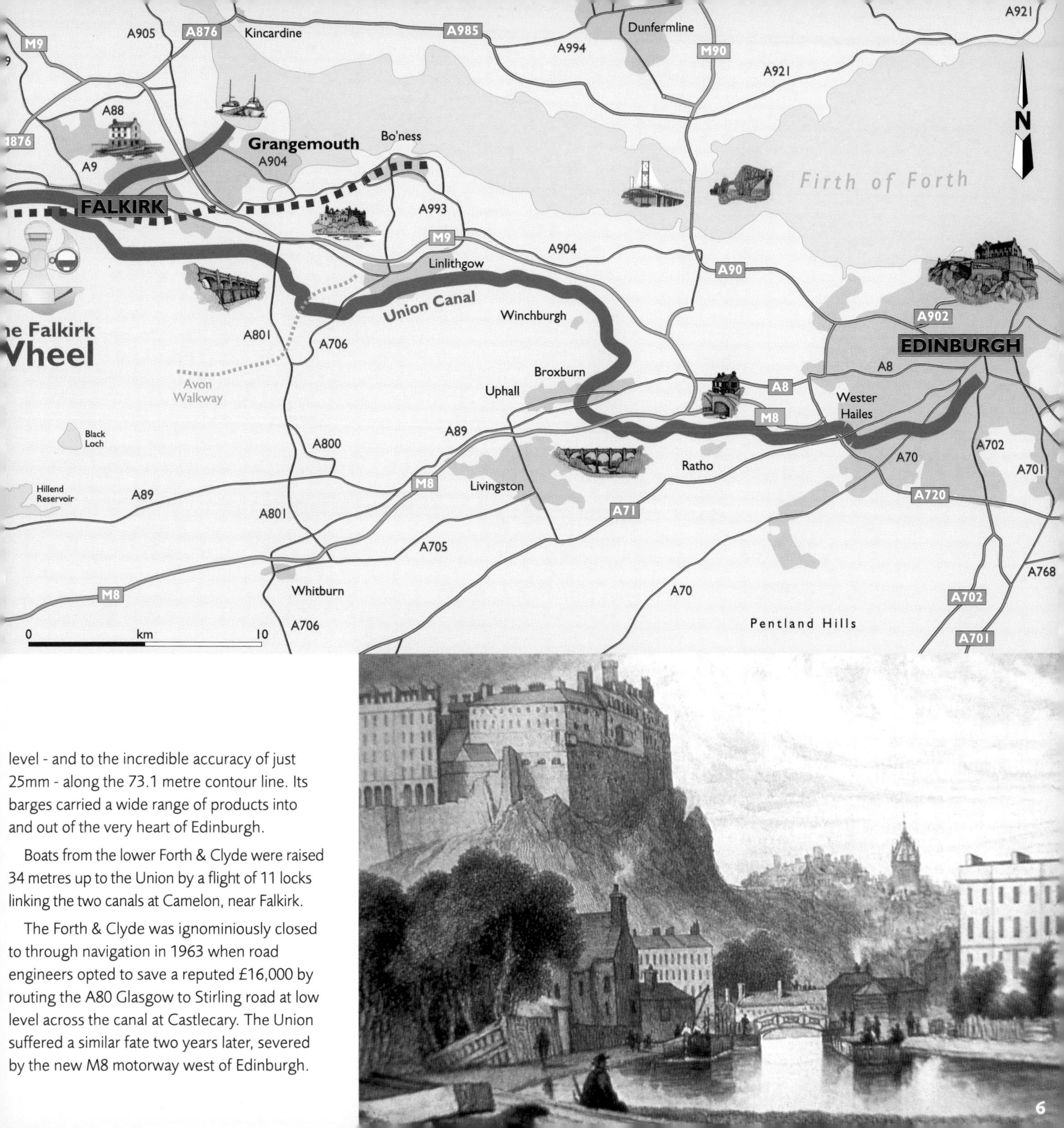

level - and to the incredible accuracy of just 25mm - along the 73.1 metre contour line. Its barges carried a wide range of products into and out of the very heart of Edinburgh.

Boats from the lower Forth & Clyde were raised 34 metres up to the Union by a flight of 11 locks linking the two canals at Camelon, near Falkirk.

The Forth & Clyde was ignominiously closed to through navigation in 1963 when road engineers opted to save a reputed £16,000 by routing the A80 Glasgow to Stirling road at low level across the canal at Castlecary. The Union suffered a similar fate two years later, severed by the new M8 motorway west of Edinburgh.

STRANGE BUT TRUE

Canal water from the Forth & Clyde was regularly abstracted during the 1800s and used as untreated drinking water for the local population. Among the main recipients were staff and patients at Glasgow's Royal Infirmary.

Courtesy Falkirk Museums

STRANGE BUT TRUE

Goldfish flourished in the Forth & Clyde's unusually warm waters alongside the Singer sewing machine works at Clydebank. Canal water had been abstracted for use in what was then the World's largest factory and returned to the Forth & Clyde at a higher temperature.

Scotland's earliest canal, The Forth & Clyde, was completed in 1790 and quickly established itself as a major transport route, providing a vital artery for the development of the central belt.

As also the World's first sea to sea ship canal, its tall - masted ships demanded bridges that swung or lifted open as cargoes, including sugar, timber and grain, sailed through 40 locks, right across Scotland to and from Baltic ports or the Western Isles.

The canal opened up regular services to far flung places like Hamburg, St.Petersburg and Trieste. Beside its towpath new industries, such as boat building, munitions factories, brickworks and distilleries, soon flourished.

The shorter Edinburgh and Glasgow Union Canal was opened 32 years later towards the end of the canal building era; cut all on one level with no locks at all along its main length.

Its horse-pulled barges ferried coal, stone and even manure beneath fixed arch bridges and across spectacular aqueducts to the homes, factories and farms of 19th Century Edinburgh.

With roads just rough tracks, and railways still being invented, these bustling waterways were the motorways of their age - the country's first commercial transport network. By the 1830s up to 200,000 passengers travelled the route annually.

Daytrippers 'took the air' journeying on pleasure steamers, and a considerable proportion of the route's annual three million tonnes of cargo was transported the full distance between Glasgow and Edinburgh via the flight of 11 locks linking the two canals near Falkirk.

EDINBURGH

AND

GLASGOW.

THE FORTH & CLYDE

AND UNION CANAL

PASSAGE BOAT,

SWIFT.

ntil the SECOND LIGHT PASSAGE BOAT ow building at *Tophill*, near *Port-Downie* is finish-d, the SWIFT will sail as follows:—

FROM

Port-Dundas, Glasgow,

very MONDAY, WEDNESDAY, & FRIDAY,

At half-past Seven o'Clock Morning.

FROM

Port-Hopetoun, Edinburgh,

very TUESDAY, THURSDAY, & SATURDAY,

At Eight o'Clock Morning.

anal Office, Port-Dundas,
GLASGOW, 19th November, 1833.

Aitken & Co. Printers.

Courtesy Falkirk Museums

STRANGE BUT TRUE

Slimline 'swiftboats', pulled only by the fastest horses and carrying 60 passengers, each paying 4 shillings (20 pence) a trip, operated an express service between Glasgow and Edinburgh, with the journey taking just over seven hours. A scythe, projecting from the boat's prow, would cut through the tow line of any slow moving vessels which failed to give way. At Falkirk's flight of locks, passengers saved time by changing boats.

Sale
Save 50%

STRANGE BUT TRUE

Keystones on the Union Canal's Laughin' and Greetin' Bridge are carved with a laughing face on one side and a sad one on the other. This reflects the successful builder who cut an easy stretch of canal one side of the bridge, and the unfortunate one who nearly went bankrupt digging a tunnel on the other side.

the race to refurbish

When engineers arrived to refurbish the two derelict canals, they were met by a route obstructed in 32 places by infilled bridges or pipelines. Most of the locks, bridges and aqueducts needed at least some repair work.

The challenges of raising all the finance meant refurbishment was now starting two years late. Original completion dates, on which much of the funding depended, had though still to be met; so the intended five year rescue programme had to be cut to three.

All 32 major blockages had to be removed. Planning and programming this restoration work, without affecting the canals' vital performance as drainage channels, proved a significant logistical exercise.

At Wester Hailes in Edinburgh, a new 1.7km length of the Union Canal had to be cut as the original route had long since been infilled. In Glasgow's suburbs, three buried Forth & Clyde locks were unearthed and restored, while eight new ones have been built near Falkirk.

Apprentices from Heritage Agency, Historic Scotland, even reproduced missing milestones and placed them along the side of the Union Canal.

STRANGE BUT TRUE

Nineteenth Century bodysnatchers Burke and Hare worked as navvies building the Union Canal; later using it to quickly transport their gruesome 'swag' from nearby graveyards.

WILLIAM BURKE

WILLIAM HARE

Artist: J.R. after Lutenor, courtesy Scottish National Portrait Gallery

STRANGE BUT TRUE

During dredging work, rare plants were protected by an abundant supply of old supermarket trolleys retrieved from the canals.

keeping the water flowing

The Forth & Clyde transfers some 40 million litres of water every day as its route drops 47 metres down to each coastline through some 20 locks either side of its highest level, known in canal circles as the Summit Pound.

This 30km stretch of level canal, centred on Kirkintilloch, is replenished daily with water drawn from a complex interconnected network involving 10 reservoirs. Gauges along the canal route indicate when water levels need topping up and sluice gates are opened in the upland reservoirs.

The Union Canal is a rare 'all on one level' contour canal with no locks along its main length. It needs a lower volume of top up water drawn from Cobbinshaw Reservoir, West Lothian.

The canal has spectacular aqueducts across the rivers Avon and Almond and at Slateford near Edinburgh.

Both canals flourished until the First World War when Grangemouth docks, the route's important eastern sea link into the Firth of Forth, was closed as a security measure. Their role as transport corridors rapidly declined, taken over by the growing railway network.

The axe fell in the 1960s when new roads and motorways were built across both canals at low level, brutally severing them as navigation routes.

The future use of a limited headroom Forth & Clyde, with its sea going vessels, was not foreseen. So, in 1963, the A80 road was designed to cross the canal on embankment instead of incorporating a more expensive bridge option. A similar fate, involving the M8 motorway, killed off the Union Canal a couple of years later.

For decades the canals lay virtually abandoned, maintained only for safety and to allow their role as vital land drains to continue. Bridges were filled in, crumbling lock gates let

the water through without the need for lock keepers. The waterways seemed forgotten.

The mid 1970s saw renewed interest, led mainly by the voluntary sector and canal enthusiasts, in the use of water routes this time for leisure activities. British Waterways began to realise its liabilities could be turned into assets, as catalysts encouraging canalside development, and gradually the tide started turning.

In Scotland, two initiatives - the Glasgow and the West Lothian Canal projects - were completed during the early 1990s, removing four obstructions to navigation along the route.

The arrival in 1994 of the lottery funded Millennium Commission opened up even further opportunities. Scottish Enterprise, European agencies and local councils all rallied round to help raise the finance needed for a British Waterways led scheme to revitalise the full length of the two canals.

STRANGE BUT TRUE

To celebrate reopening of the Forth & Clyde Canal in 2001, Prince Charles poured a hogshead full of water from the River Clyde into the Firth of Forth. This re-enacted - in reverse - a 1790 ceremony marking completion of the F&C, the World's first sea to sea ship canal, when a hogshead of River Forth water was tipped into the Clyde to commemorate 'connection of the eastern and western seas'.

Public support was high. When the project was threatened with cancellation, volunteers collected over 30,000 signatures petitioning for it to be given the go ahead.

Yet the task of raising the required £84.5 million still proved challenging and, by the time funds were finally on the table, a planned five year reconstruction programme had to be achieved in only three.

At construction sites across Scotland an army of 700 modernday 'navvies' - the description used for the original builders of 'navigable' waterways - constructed new timber lock gates and abseiled down the sides of aqueducts to return a route - all of which was a Scheduled Ancient Monument - back to its former glory.

When Her Majesty the Queen officially opened The Millennium Link in May 2002, the first seeds of canalside redevelopment were already bearing fruit. New houses with 'canal views' sold rapidly. Developers of flats, offices and pubs vied with each other for the increasingly lucrative waterside sites.

At Kirkintilloch, a rubbish strewn canal basin of stagnant water had been replaced by a roadside sign proclaiming the town 'Scotland's Canal Capital'. Half of an estimated £400 million of private sector investment, expected to be generated by the new waterway, had already been promised; bringing with it much needed optimism and employment. And all along the waterway's rebuilt towpath, 'The People's Project' was rapidly coming alive.

THE FORTH & CLYDE CANAL

- The World's first sea to sea ship canal.
- 61km long, with 38 operating locks, 38 bridges and 25 aqueducts.
- Built 1768 - 1790 by engineers John Smeaton and Robert Whitworth.

THE UNION CANAL

- A rare contour canal built on one level.
- Built 1818 -1822 by engineer Hugh Baird.
- Originally 51km long with 84 bridges - 62 of them arch bridges - 24 aqueducts, Scotland's only canal tunnel, but no locks (though the flight of 11 at Falkirk was officially still on the Union Canal). Completion of The Falkirk Wheel site extended the Union Canal by 2km and added three locks, two more bridges, two aqueducts, another canal tunnel and the Wheel itself.

the environmental artery - so much to see for free

The Lowland Canals are one of Scotland's most important environmental corridors, rich in wildlife and aquatic plants. The overall route, though a relatively small wetland area compared to Scotland's many rivers and lochs, offers a unique combination of shallow, stable, slow flowing and nutrient rich water, well aerated as it falls over numerous lock gates.

This regime supports a large and impressive range of wetland plants, invertebrates, amphibians, birds and mammals in and around the canals.

Stretching coast to coast, and invading the catchments of both the Rivers Forth and Clyde, the canals act as an environmental artery. They form vital links between isolated wildlife areas and offer a range of different habitats in which plants and animals flourish.

The result is a rare combination of over 300 plant species, and the animals that depend on them, all accessible in reasonably close proximity. The creation of several nature conservation sites along or near the canals is recognition of their wildlife value.

The water is home to over 30 varieties of aquatic plants; 15 species of mollusc; 33 different types of water flea and even freshwater sponges. Invertebrates, sporting such intriguing names as the 'wandering snail' or 'greater ramshorn', inhabit the canal bed.

Pike, roach, perch, eels and even brown trout share the water with mallard, coots and, curiously, red-eared terrapins sporting an up to 100 year lifespan and thought to be long abandoned pets.

Lurking in bankside vegetation are 'lesser water boatmen' and beetles of every variety except Liverpudlian singers. Many of the plants near the canal edge, like the stress-relieving valerian, were used as herbal remedies long before the days of the National Health Service.

Rare and protected plants include Bennett's pondweed, Tufted Loosestrife and Royal Fern. Otters, bats, mink, water voles and roe deer have all been sighted and mute swans regularly nest alongside the canal.

Why not take your own wildlife safari along the many kilometres of readily accessible towpath.

DATES

1768	Forth & Clyde Canal started at the foot of Grange Burn
1790	Forth & Clyde Canal fully opened
1818 - 1822	Union Canal built
1933	Falkirk Locks closed and built over
1963	Forth & Clyde Canal closed to through navigation
1965	Union Canal similarly closed.
1999 - 2001	Both canals refurbished
2000 - 2002	The Falkirk Wheel built

24 May 2002 The Millennium Link opened by The Queen

British
Waterways
Scotland
welcome to
The Falkirk
Wheel

FORTH & CLYD

The Falkirk Wheel - the making of a landmark

The Falkirk Wheel is unique. Not only is it the first boatlift of its type anywhere, but its combination of engineering ingenuity and architectural imagination creates both an eyecatching working sculpture and Scotland's most unusual tourist attraction.

During the structure's five year design period the boatlift developed from a seesaw style lift, based on ancient Greek technology, to a circular turning wheel. The end result, today's dramatic 21st Century shape, is surely the most appropriate way to celebrate Britain's new canal era.

The Wheel has already claimed its place as a major Scottish landmark and is one of the World's most important canal structures.

The way its computer controlled machinery gracefully raises or lowers 500 tonnes of boats and water the 25 metre difference between two canals appears complex; but is deceptively simple.

As you experience the journey through a canal tunnel and across an aqueduct - before seeming to drop off the end as your boat is lowered by the Wheel - you will be enjoying the most memorable yet gentle of white knuckle rides.

To route both the Union Canal, and the Forth & Clyde 35 metres below it, into the Wheel complex involved cutting a new canal section, building three locks, two aqueducts, two bridges and excavating Britain's first canal tunnel for over 100 years.

A 1km extension of the Union Canal ends in a double staircase lock, which lowers boats 7 metres to a holding basin. From here they pass beneath a bridge carrying the main Edinburgh to Glasgow rail line and enter a 168 metre long canal tunnel driven beneath the Roman Antonine Wall.

Boats emerge to cross a 104 metre long aqueduct which runs directly onto the Wheel's upper gondola.

With up to four boats at a time sealed into the gondola behind a pair of flap gates, the Wheel's actual travel time, down to a dry well alongside the lower basin, takes about five minutes.

Similar gates release boats into the basin where, through a single lock, they drop the final 3 metres to join the Forth & Clyde Canal.

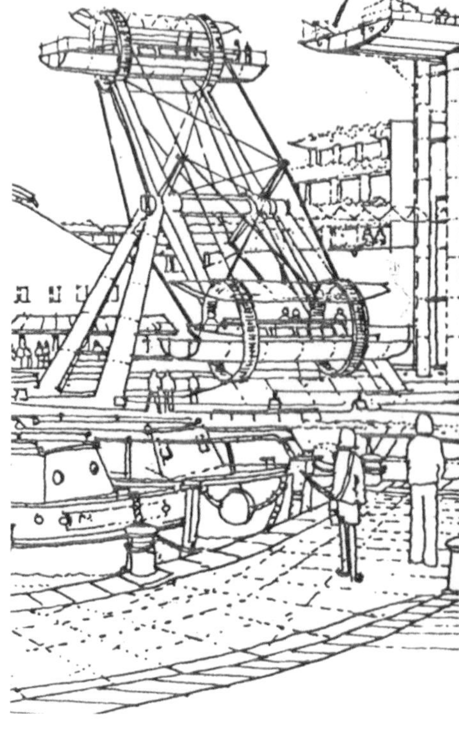

Hidden in a wood near Falkirk are the remains of an old, half buried canal lock. This is all that is visible of the Wheel's predecessor - a flight of 11 locks, the rest of which lie, long forgotten, beneath nearby streets.

Until 1933, this impressive group of locks linked the Union Canal with the Forth & Clyde Canal, 34 metres below and all but a day's heavy work away opening and closing some 44 lock gates.

Following the locks' closure, the two canals continued - separately - a spiral of decline and virtual abandonment. Their revival, early in 2002, as part of The Millennium Link Project, demanded a new connection.

In 1994, Dundee based architect Nicoll Russell Studios was asked to develop, along with British Waterways, fresh and exciting ideas worthy of a structure that was recognised from the outset as having the potential to become an international landmark.

The site chosen was a steep sloping field on the outskirts of Falkirk, home of a redundant tarworks some 3km from where the original locks lie buried.

But what form of structure should be built?

A vast spoon - shaped seesaw, a vertical lift concealed within a cylindrical waterfall, even an overhead monorail system incorporating tilting tanks, were some of the initial doodles on designers' notepads.

The first conceptual design was based on the Greek Noria machine - a giant tipping lift used to irrigate fields.This later evolved into an open cylindrical drum containing rotating gondolas to carry the boats.

By 1999, the challenges of making this difficult concept workable had led to a fairground style ferris wheel with four hanging, rather than rotating, gondolas. This was the design originally intended to be built.

the boatlift's development - from tilting tanks to a rotating wheel

Early ideas for connecting the canals ranged from an overhead monorail with the boats carried beneath in tilting tanks, to a funicular railway or giant seesaw. Turning counterweighted arms, or hefty cranes, were imagined, raising and lowering the boats between canals.

During the five year design stage, the concept of a turning wheel was developed, first as an open cylindrical drum. This later became a 19th Century style ferris wheel with four hanging gondolas. The appreciation that a wheel does not also demand a rim, led to today's striking design.

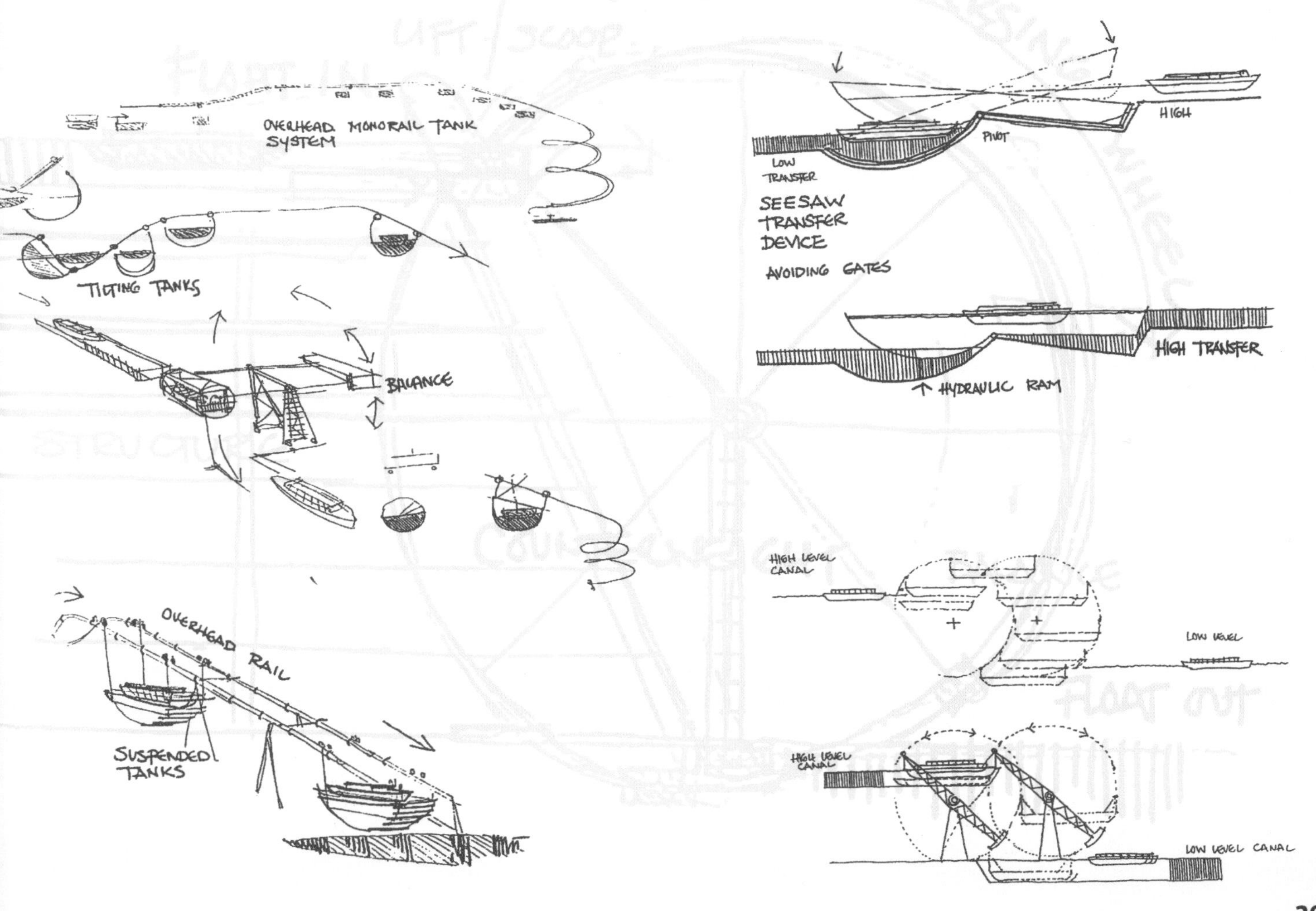

BURIED LOCKS

It took virtually a full day for boats and their owners to negotiate the Wheel's predecessor - a flight of 11 locks, abandoned in 1933 and now buried beneath Falkirk streets. Descending the 34 metre drop between the two canals used up 3500 tonnes of water every trip, and reservoirs were needed beside the locks to replenish supplies. By contrast, The Falkirk Wheel uses no water and the same journey takes 15 minutes.

Courtesy Falkirk Museums

However, with a construction company chosen, British Waterways felt that this somewhat clumsy looking design could be improved to create a more modern structure worthy of celebrating a new Millennium. A hectic month of meetings followed as a 20 strong team of engineers, architects and steelwork fabricators brainstormed their way through yet more ideas.

The result has won design awards worldwide. Yet there are as many ways to describe what its shape represents as there are people asked. Most images encompass Scottish or marine architectural themes. But take your pick from; Celtic inspired double - headed axes, the spine of a fish, ribcage of a whale, or the vast turning propellers of a Clydebank built ship.

Whatever you want the structure to resemble, 35 lorry loads of it were delivered to the site from a Derbyshire steelworks in Summer 2001. Major parts of the Wheel had earlier been painstakingly assembled and bolted together in the factory, like a giant Meccano set, to ensure a perfect fit.

Sections were then taken apart again and reduced to sizes suitable for transporting by road to Falkirk. There they were once more bolted together on the ground before a massive crane positioned the Wheel's five major components.

All this bolting and unbolting helped the construction team assemble some 1200 tonnes of steel, plus two 50 tonne gondolas, to an accuracy of just 10mm.

The completed Wheel lies at the end of a reinforced concrete aqueduct which is linked, via a tunnel and a double staircase lock, to the Union Canal. Boats entering the Wheel's upper gondola are lowered, along with the water they float in, to the basin below. At the same time an equal weight of boats and water rises up in the other gondola.

A series of five cogs helps ensure that the gondolas always remain horizontal; and the totally balanced Wheel is turned so efficiently by a group of hydraulic motors, that the electricity cost needed for one half revolution is just a few pence.

Everything is computer controlled - even water levels in the aqueduct and lower basin - but the Wheel's mechanics involve only proven, fail safe engineering. It is the way this technology has been cleverly combined into one structure that also makes The Falkirk Wheel unique.

precision engineering - big scale

Although centre stage, the 1800 tonne Wheel costs about quarter of the overall £20 million price tag for The Falkirk Wheel complex with its aqueduct, tunnel, canal extension and locks.

Main components of the Wheel were trial assembled at steel fabricator, Butterley Engineering's, Derbyshire factory to check everything fitted, and then bolted together again on site prior to lifting into position.

This attention to detail meant that the planned week long erection operation was completed a day early. Components were generally positioned to an accuracy of 10mm, with the 25 metre long axle section aligned to just 1mm.

As the Wheel turns, stresses imposed on the structure by the total 600 tonne weight of water-filled gondolas change completely in direction. Instead of using normal welded joints, steel sections were bolted together, making them more robust to resist fatigue induced stresses.

This gave the construction team the awesome task of mating 15,000 bolts with over 45,000 bolt holes.

how the wheel works

Turning the Wheel involves two simple engineering functions brought together as an innovative, energy saving combination.

The prime mechanism is a series of hydraulic motors that rotate the 4 metre diameter central axle and the two propeller-shaped arms fixed to it. Helping to keep the gondolas, and the boats inside them, horizontal throughout the operation is the second mechanism - a row of linked cogs that interact as the wheel turns, but need no power supply.

The ten hydraulic motors are positioned around a fixed plate behind the axle. As an outer ring of teeth on each motor rotates, it engages with similar teeth on the axle rim, turning the axle and, with it, the entire Wheel.

One half revolution, moving boats between the two canals, takes less then five minutes. Though, with boats loading and unloading, total journey time is around 15 minutes.

As both 50 tonne gondolas contain the same 250 tonne weight of water and boats, the perfectly balanced Wheel needs only 1.5kW hours of electricity - costing just a few pence - to complete a half turn. The really clever bit though is ensuring that the 25 metre long gondolas - supported at each end inside holes in the main propeller arms - always remain horizontal.

As the arms turn, bogie wheels, fixed beneath the ends of each gondola, run around a single curved rail attached to the inside rim of the hole in each arm. In theory this should be sufficient to keep the gondolas level.

But wheel friction in the bogies, or any sudden movement of so much water, could result in a gondola sticking or tilting. To ensure this could never happen, and the water and boats always remain level throughout the turning cycle, a row of linked cogs acts as a fail-safe backup.

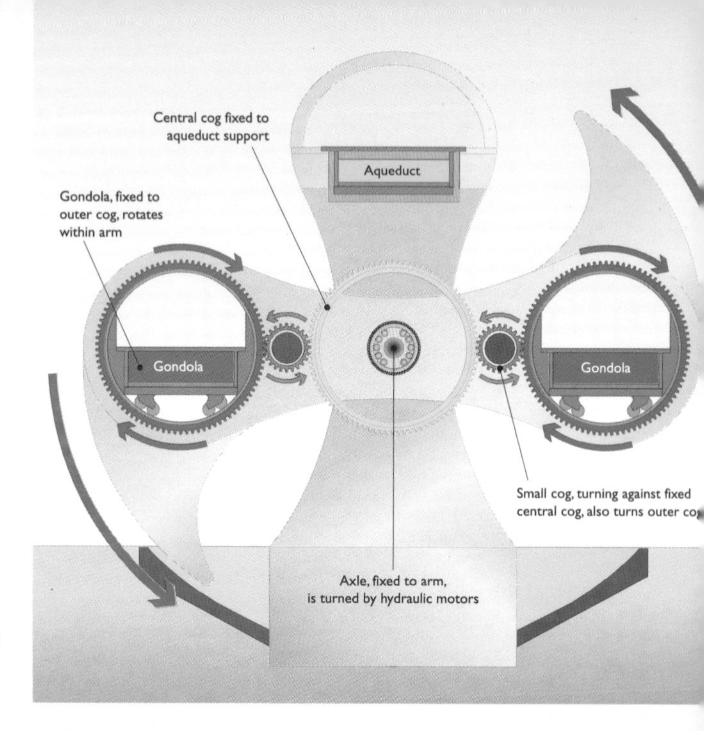

One end of each gondola is fixed to the large outside cogs in this row of five, which is hidden behind the arm nearest the aqueduct. These outer 8 metre diameter cogs are exactly the same size as the central one in the row, which is attached to the aqueduct's support column and cannot turn. Two smaller cogs, attached to the arm, lie between these larger ones to link all five.

When the Wheel rotates, these small cogs move with it and their toothed edges turn against both the fixed central cog and the outer ones to which the gondolas are joined.

With these large cogs all the same size, the attached gondolas rotate at the exact same speed as the Wheel - but in the opposite direction. In other words, the gondolas are always horizontal no matter where the Wheel is in its cycle.

Simple, safe, innovative and energy free.

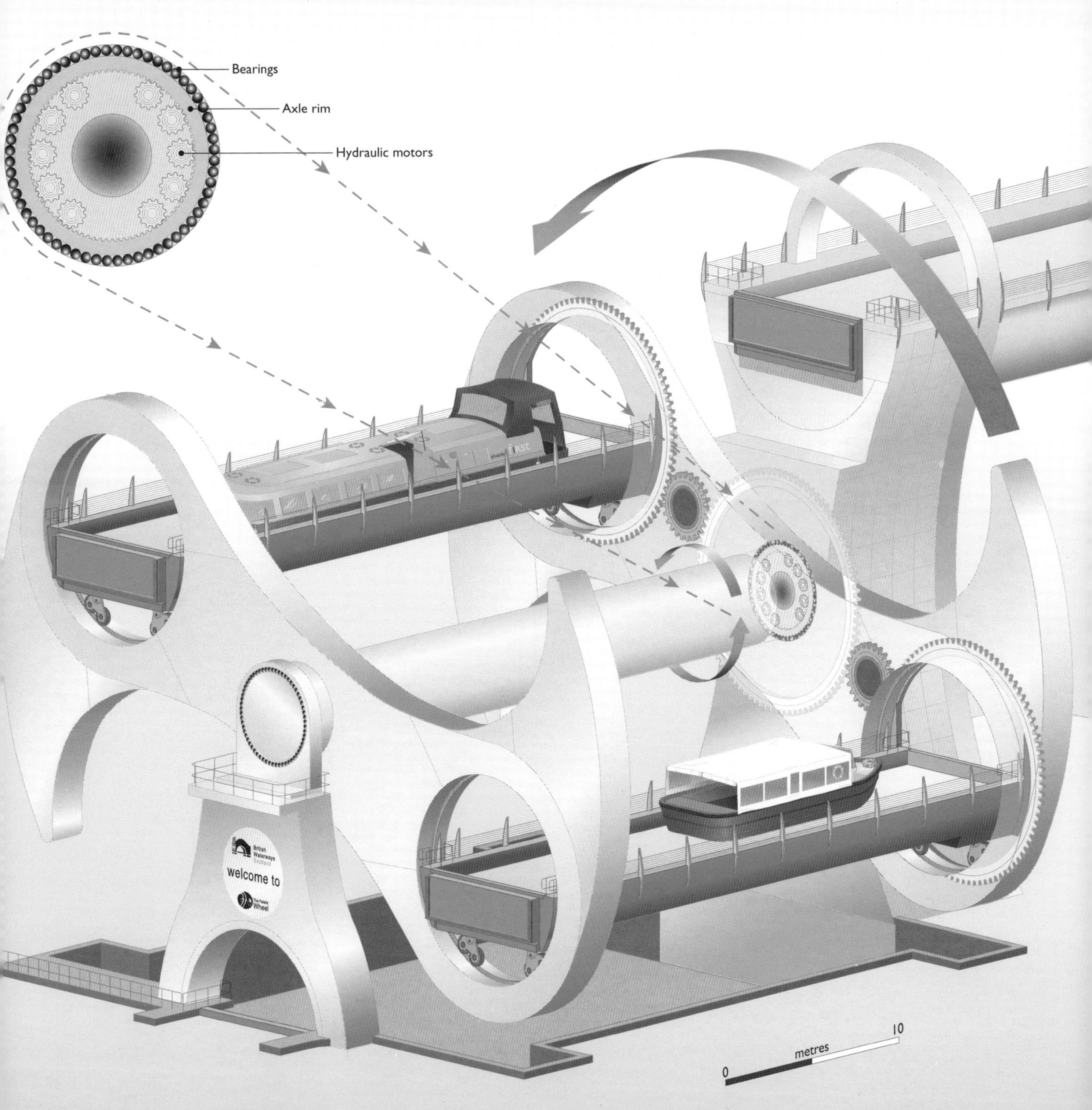
Bearings
Axle rim
Hydraulic motors
British Waterways Scotland
welcome to
The Falkirk Wheel
0
metres
10

TRUE OR FALSE?

If there are four boats in one gondola, and none in the other, the Wheel will be out of balance and cannot turn.

FALSE: Remember Archimedes' Principle. Each boat displaces its exact own weight of water as it enters the gondola. So, assuming water depth is the same, each gondola will transport the same total load, 250 tonnes, no matter how many boats - or fish - it contains.

close the gate

Steel gates at both ends of the gondolas, and where they dock with the aqueduct and lower basin, tilt open or shut hydraulically. As a gondola arrives, a rubber seal springs out across the bottom and sides of the 50mm wide air gap between it and either the aqueduct or lower basin. Water is pumped into the much larger gap between the end gates on either structure, equalising levels, before both gates fold down flat to allow boats in or out.

The sequence is then reversed, with both gate rotating up to the vertical again, the gap between them pumped dry and the rubber seal retracted hydraulically, allowing the gondola to be raised or lowered as the Wheel turns.

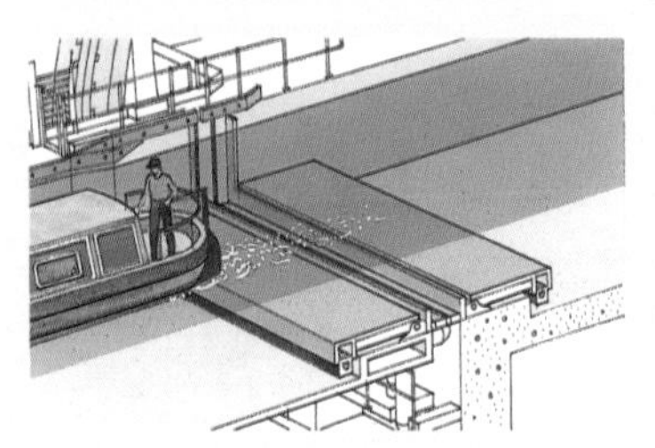

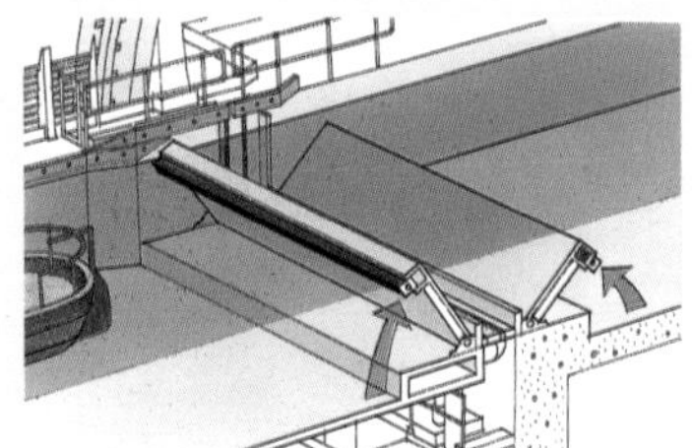

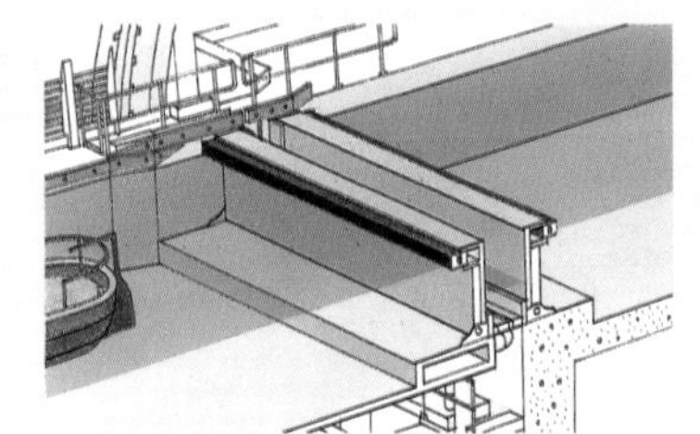

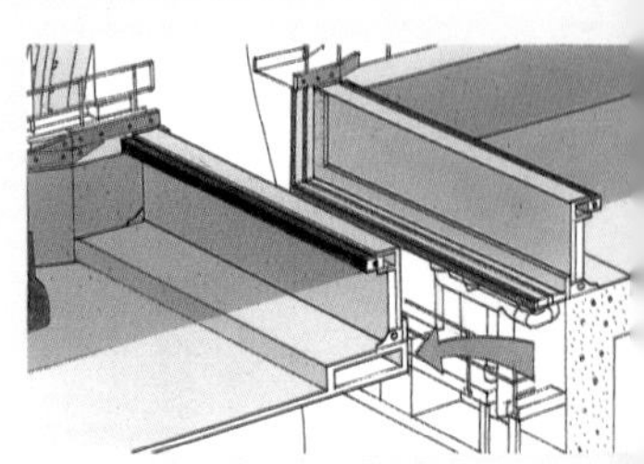

illustrated by Brian De

depth control

The secret of the boatlift's smooth, economic operation is aiming to ensure that both loaded gondolas weigh virtually the same, so that the Wheel remains balanced.

Archimedes Principle guarantees that, as a boat enters the gondola, it displaces exactly its own weight in water. So, regardless of whether gondolas are empty or full of boats, they will be carrying the same load.

The only variable able to create an imbalance is differing water depths and it is essential gondolas contain very nearly the same level of water. This is dependent on water levels in both the aqueduct and lower basin, themselves influence by locks at the site's entry and exit points.

Water levels throughout the complex are monitored and controlled around the clock by an extensive network of sensors, valves and hidden bypass pipes.

State of the art computer software records water depth to a few millimetres, and allows only a maximum 75mm difference between levels in each gondola.

The computers can even predict if tolerance are likely to be exceeded and take early preventative action.

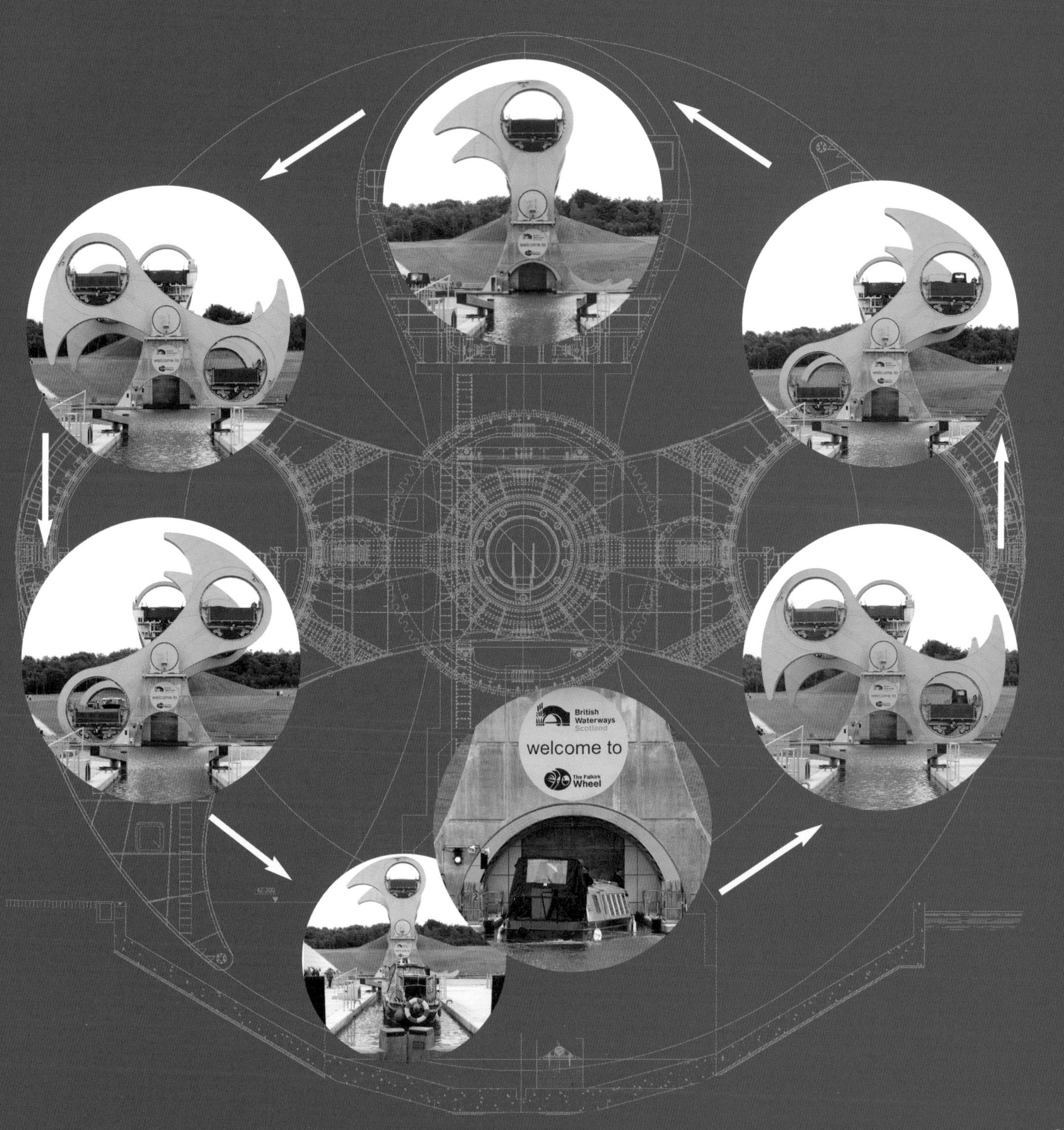
British
Waterways
Scotland
welcome to
The Falkirk
Wheel

STRANGE BUT TRUE

- The Wheel site attracts an increasing number of Glaswegian fish, crowding into its lower basin. The more adventurous take the lift up to the Union Canal and complete their journey east towards Edinburgh.
- Engineers building the Wheel had to match 15,000 bolts with 45,000 bolt holes. The pile of waste metal punched out to make the holes weighed 7 tonnes.

fly through aqueduct

The architectural concept of the 104 metre long aqueduct, with its trough appearing to 'fly' through circular hoops, created challenges for the structure's designers.

Note how the trough is connected only at two points around the hoops and imagine the high loads passing through this small area of concrete, which needs to be heavily reinforced with numerous steel bars.

The upper half of each hoop is hollow, made not of concrete but lightweight glass reinforced plastic.

THE FALKIRK WHEEL

- The World's first rotating boatlift, 35 metres high and 27 metres long. The total connection cost £20 million to build and was opened in 2002.
- The Wheel weighs 1200 tonnes, plus two 50 tonne gondolas. Each gondola transfers a total 250 tonnes of boats and water the 25 metre vertical distance between the Union and Forth & Clyde Canals.
- Boat journeys through the Wheel take 15 minutes overall; but it completes its half turn between the two canal heights in just five minutes.

tunnel vision

Britain's first new canal tunnel for over a century was built to route boats beneath the Roman remains of the Antonine Wall. No ground disturbance was allowed near this earth wall, so the 168 metre long tunnel was excavated very carefully in three horizontal stages.

As upper sections of rock were removed, the sides and roof of the tunnel were sprayed with a 300mm thick layer of concrete, reinforced with steel mesh, to provide immediate support.

To excavate the bottom of the tunnel, rock was sliced away horizontally by a massive 'planing' machine similar to those used to remove the top surface of a road. Excavated rock was reused to form the adjacent embankment linking the tunnel to the aqueduct.

The tunnel floor is formed of 600mm thick reinforced concrete to support it over old fireclay mine workings beneath.

the antonine wall

The Wheel shares its site with another important engineering structure that pre-dates it by a mere 1800 years - The Antonine Wall. Once the Roman's most northerly frontier of its Empire, only an outline now remains of this 4 metre high earth mound with its deep ditch on the northern flank.

Built by Emperor Antoninus Pius in AD 142, the turf covered wall, with large cobbled foundations, boasted regular forts along its 60km length between the rivers Clyde and Forth. Eighteenth Century navvies, cutting the Forth and Clyde Canal, incorporated sections of the wall's ditch into its route.

Today's visitors are welcome to inspect the wall, but the Romans found it difficult to defend from marauding Picts and abandoned the structure after just 60 years. They retreated south to the more substantial defence, Hadrian's Wall.

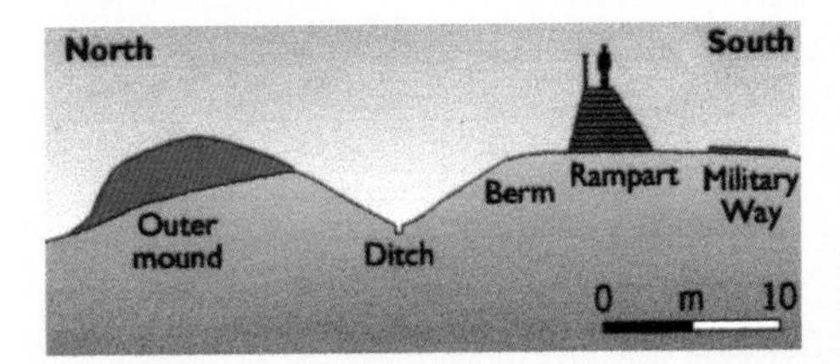

turn so

xperience
rk

PROJECT FINANCE

The £84.5 million Millennium Link's funding partnership includes;

Millennium Commission: £33.8 million
Scottish Enterprise: £18.7 million
British Waterways: £16.1 million
European Union: £8.6 million
Seven local councils: £7.3 million

FALKIRK WHEEL CONSTRUCTION TEAM

Client: British Waterways Scotland

Conceptual design: Nicoll Russell Studios/ British Waterways Scotland

Main contractor: Morrison Construction - Bachy Soletanche Joint Venture

Wheel steelwork: fabricator and erector: Butterley Engineering

Wheel and aqueduct architect: RMJM

Civil and structural engineering designer: Arup Consultants and Tony Gee & Partners

Mechanical engineering designer: Bennett Associates

Control systems: design and installation: Fairfield Controls

a catalyst for the future - unlocking Scotland's potential

The Millennium Link, with The Falkirk Wheel at its centre, is a win win project for Scotland.

The Wheel, with its built in 'wow' factor and offer of a somewhat novel white knuckle ride, is already a top tourist attraction. The Millennium Link Project has become a new coast to coast pleasure waterway, offering wide-ranging leisure facilities.

Where work-horses once filled the towpaths, families and cyclists have taken their place.

Sea-going yachts and hundreds of brightly coloured canal boats are replacing 19th Century coal barges and cargo-laden sailing ships.

Yet Scotland's new canal age is also bringing its waterways full circle in their role as commercial corridors.

Beneath those same towpaths, a network of fibre optic cables stretches across the country. Canal water is being sold to industry, and the whole canal route acts as a catalyst for waterside redevelopment.

Unemployment along this central Scotland belt had been 30% above the country's average. Within a few years this new 'ribbon of opportunity' aims to attract £400 million of private sector investment and create 4500 new jobs.

The Millennium Link and The Falkirk Wheel really are "Projects for the People".